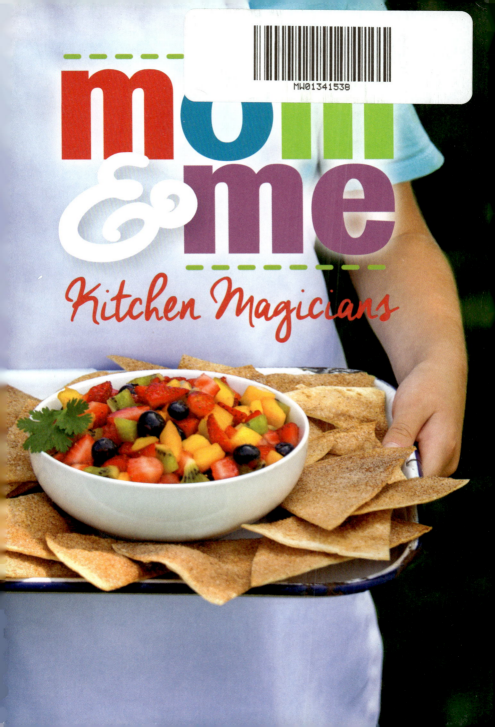

LET THE COOKING ADVENTURES BEGIN!

A lot of magic happens in the kitchen, from bread dough that mysteriously puffs up with heat to soft mixtures that turn solid in the freezer. And there's creative magic as kids turn ordinary food into personal creations they'll love to eat. But the real magic is making delicious memories together and helping little minds grow through experimenting, touching, tasting, watching, and smelling.

To make the most of your magical moments, be encouraging. Stay positive. Listen and explain. Most of all, have fun! The skills and cooking confidence your wee chefs gain will stay with them for a lifetime. It really is magic.

Copyright © 2017 CQ Products
All rights reserved.
No part of this book may be reproduced or transmitted in any form or by any means, electronic or mechanical, including photocopying, recording or by any information storage and retrieval system, without permission in writing from the publisher.

ISBN-13: 978-1-56383-597-1
Item #6225

**Printed in the USA
by G&R Publishing Co.**

Distributed By:

507 Industrial Street
Waverly, IA 50677

www.cqbookstore.com

gifts@cqbookstore.com

 CQ Products

 CQ Products

 @cqproducts

 @cqproducts

MAKING KITCHEN MAGIC

- Be prepared for messes – have clean-up supplies handy.
- Let kids do as much as their skills allow. Demonstrate how to do a task first and then let them try.
- Watch closely to see if your mini chefs can manage a task. If it's too hard or frustrating for them, move on to something else.
- Train kids to cut with butter knives before allowing them to cut with a paring knife. Cutting, grating, peeling, and using sharp utensils require close supervision.
- Help kids recognize what's hot, what's sharp, and what they shouldn't eat *(like raw meat or eggs that could make them sick)*.

HELP 2- TO 5-YEAR-OLDS WORK ON THESE SKILLS:

Scrub fresh produce in the sink; tear food into small pieces; sprinkle, brush, roll, or crush foods; knead and flatten dough; use cookie cutters; count, assemble, scoop, stir, squeeze, spread, pour, and mash foods.

IN ADDITION, 6- TO 9-YEAR-OLDS CAN GENERALLY:

Cut and dice; grate cheese and veggies; peel fruits and vegetables; crack eggs; scoop batter; grease pans; use measuring spoons and cups correctly; rinse things using a strainer; use an electric mixer with help; skewer food; use a pizza cutter and rolling pin; measure with a ruler; sift; help you with stovetop tasks.

Makes 8

PITA PILLOWS

You'll Need

2 C. all-purpose flour
1 C. whole wheat flour
1½ tsp. salt
1 (.25 oz.) pkg. instant yeast
2 T. olive oil

1 T. honey or sugar
1¼ to 1½ C. water *(at room temperature)*
Baking stone *(recommended)*

1. Put both flours, salt, and yeast in a big bowl. Add the oil, honey, and 1¼ C. water and stir with a big spoon until a ball of dough forms, adding a little more water if you need it.

Level off flour and other dry ingredients when measuring.

2. Knead the dough on a floured board for 10 minutes. Shape into a ball and set in an oiled bowl; roll the dough around in the bowl until coated. Cover with a damp towel and let rise in a warm place for 1½ hours or until doubled in size.

3. Punch down the dough with your fist and then cut it into eight even pieces. Roll each piece into a smooth ball and set on a cookie sheet; cover and let rest 20 minutes. Meanwhile, preheat your oven to 400° with a baking stone inside.

4. Flatten each ball with your hands or a rolling pin until it's ⅛" to ¼" thick; let rest 5 or 10 minutes. Carefully set a few pitas at a time on the hot baking stone **(adult's job)**. Bake 4 to 6 minutes or until lightly browned and puffed up like a pillow. *Mmm-agical!* Cool before cutting in half; fill with your favorite sandwich fixings.

MAKES 8

FROZEN BANANA POPS

4 bananas, peeled
1¼ C. milk chocolate chips
1 T. coconut oil
Candy sprinkles
Spray whipped cream
Maraschino cherries
Chocolate graham cracker crumbs
Mini peanut butter cups, mini and regular M&Ms, and/or other candies
Mini marshmallows
8 popsicle sticks

1 Cut each banana in half and insert a popsicle stick in cut ends. Freeze on a parchment paper-lined pan for 2 hours.

2 Melt chocolate chips and oil in the microwave, stirring every 30 seconds until smooth.

3 Sundae Pops: Dip frozen bananas halfway in melted chocolate and immediately coat the top half with sprinkles; freeze 15 minutes. To serve, top with whipped cream and a cherry.

4 Bearbana: Coat frozen bananas with melted chocolate and roll in chocolate graham cracker crumbs. Use melted chocolate to attach a peanut butter cup snout, halved *(flattened)* mini marshmallow eyeballs, and M&M nose, mouth, eyes, and ears, cutting in half as needed.

Use your imagination to create all kinds of banan-imals, like dogs, cats, cows, and reindeer.

Serves 6

CLUCKER NUGGETS

Line a rimmed baking sheet with parchment paper. Cut 1½ lbs. boneless, skinless chicken breasts into bite-size pieces (adult's job). Mix ¼ C. all-purpose flour and ½ tsp. each paprika and garlic powder on a plate and set aside. In a bowl, whisk 1 egg with ½ C. buttermilk. In another bowl, mix ¾ C. fine dry bread crumbs, ¼ C. each finely crushed corn flakes cereal and grated Parmesan cheese, and ¼ tsp. salt. Working with a few pieces at a time, coat chicken in flour mixture and tap off extra; then dip in the egg mixture and coat in crumbs. *(Discard any remaining dipping mixtures.)* Set on the prepped pan and chill for 30 minutes.

Preheat your oven to 375°. Spritz chicken with cooking spray and bake 20 minutes or until done. Serve with your favorite dipping sauce.

Servings vary

LUNCH SPEARS

Gather your favorite sandwich fixings. Wash some grapes and slice a peeled banana. Cut bread and cheese into 1" to 2" pieces *(use cookie cutters for fun shapes)* and cut meat into 1" ribbons or chunks. Then let the assembly begin! Try these tasty spears:

PB & J: Spread peanut butter and jelly between two slices of bread. Cut into four squares and thread on skewers with banana slices.

Meat & Cheese: Thread pieces of bread, lettuce, bacon, cheese, and deli meat *(accordion-folded)* on skewers and anchor the top and bottom with grape tomatoes or pickles.

Fruit & Cheese: Thread alternating pieces of cheese, summer sausage, and grapes on skewers.

BREAKFAST QUESADILLAS

In a medium bowl, whisk 4 eggs with salt and black pepper to taste. Coat a large skillet with cooking spray and set over medium heat *(adult's job)*. Add the eggs; cook and stir until done, then set aside. Place 2 *(8" to 10")* thin crust flatbreads *(we used multi-grain Flat Outs)* or flour tortillas on a griddle or clean skillet. Spoon eggs over half of each and sprinkle with ¼ to ½ C. shredded fontina, cheddar, or Monterey Jack cheese. Top with crumbled cooked bacon and sliced green onion. Fold the flatbreads in half over filling. Cook over medium heat, pressing down lightly, for 1 to 2 minutes on each side or until hot and melty. Serve with salsa, sour cream, or ranch dressing and sprinkle with chopped tomatoes and green onion.

ITALIAN FOIL PACKS

MAKES 4

You'll Need

- 14 to 16 oz. smoked Italian or chicken sausage
- 8 to 10 baby red potatoes
- 2 bell peppers, cored (any color)
- ¾ C. diced onion
- ¼ C. olive oil
- 1 to 1½ tsp. each dried basil, dried oregano, dried parsley, and garlic powder
- ½ tsp. each onion powder and dried thyme
- Salt and black pepper to taste
- Shredded Parmesan cheese

1 Preheat your oven to 425° and tear off 4 (18") squares of heavy-duty foil; spritz one side of each square with cooking spray.

Tie back long hair before cooking.

2 Cut the sausage into coins. Scrub and quarter the potatoes and slice the bell peppers. Combine the meat, peppers, onion, oil, and all the seasonings in a big bowl and toss together until everything is well mixed.

3 Divide the mixture evenly among the foil squares. Fold or roll the foil edges together at the top and sides to seal each pack, leaving some air space.

4 Set packs on a cookie sheet and bake about 35 minutes or until veggies are tender. Unroll the top carefully to allow steam to escape. Sprinkle with cheese and eat right out of the pack!

> *Hot steam forms inside the foil pouch to cook the food like magic. Open carefully.*

Serves 6-8

PIZZA DIP & PITA CHIPS

In a big bowl, combine 1 (14 oz.) jar meatless spaghetti sauce, 2 C. shredded mozzarella cheese, ¼ C. chopped pepperoni or Canadian bacon, ¼ C. grated Parmesan cheese, 2 tsp. dried oregano, 1 tsp. each dried basil and dried minced onion, and ¼ tsp. each garlic salt and black pepper. Stir it all up, then transfer to a small *(1½ qt.)* slow cooker. Cook on high about 1 hour, then reduce heat to low and cook 1 to 2 hours longer or until hot and melty, stirring several times. Serve from the pot or divide among small serving bowls and dip in with warm **pita chips***, breadsticks, or chunks of French bread.

* Brush olive oil over one side of 5 pita or flatbread rounds; sprinkle with sea salt, Italian seasoning, or other favorite seasonings. Cut into triangles and bake at 375° for 10 minutes, until toasted.

Makes 6-8

QUICK WAFFLED PASTRIES

Preheat your waffle iron on high, then coat with cooking spray (adult's job). For **Sweet Rolls**, open 1 (13.9 oz.) tube of refrigerated orange or cinnamon rolls and separate them, setting the frosting aside. Place a few rolls on the hot iron, leaving space between them, close the lid and press down lightly. Cook until golden brown and no longer doughy, about 2 minutes. Repeat to cook the remaining rolls. Spread the set-aside frosting over the warm rolls. Oh yum!

Make **Fruit Turnovers** the same way. Assemble the fill-and-bake cherry or apple turnovers from 1 (12 oz.) refrigerated box as directed on the package. Cook in the waffle iron until golden brown, and drizzle with the frosting.

Makes 6-8

FRUITY POPSICLES

To make a simple syrup, mix ¾ C. water and 2 T. sugar in a saucepan over medium heat and boil 4 minutes; let cool. Using a blender **(adult's job)**, puree 1 small peeled and chopped mango with 3 T. simple syrup until smooth; pour into a bowl. Rinsing the blender after each fruit, puree 50 to 60 blueberries *(let your child count them)*, 1 C. fresh raspberries *(a 6 oz. container)*, and 2 peeled sliced kiwifruit, adding 3 T. simple syrup to each batch. Pour purees into separate bowls. To make popsicles, pour a layer of one fruit puree into each popsicle mold, filling ¼ to ⅓ full. Freeze 20 minutes. One at a time, carefully add other layers of puree to each mold and freeze 15 minutes between layers. Insert sticks or handles while still slushy, then freeze overnight.

MAKES 4

LETTERS FOR LUNCH

- 1 tsp. canola oil
- ¾ C. diced ham
- 2 T. chopped onion
- ¾ C. shredded Swiss cheese
- 3 oz. cream cheese, softened
- 1 (8 oz.) tube refrigerated crescent dough sheet

1 Preheat your oven to 400°. Heat oil in a skillet over medium heat and add the ham and onion; cook until onion is tender **(adult's job)**.

2 Stir in both cheeses and cook 2 or 3 minutes more, until melted. Set aside.

3 Unroll dough and flatten slightly, making edges straight. With a pizza cutter, slice in half both ways to get four rectangles. Spoon ham mixture onto the center of each rectangle.

4 Starting with a short side, fold a third of the dough over the filling; press edges together.

5 Bring both corners of the other short side to the center to make a point; fold over like an envelope and press lightly to seal. Bake on an ungreased cookie sheet 10 to 12 minutes, until golden brown. "Deliver" the letters to serving plates.

These yummy envelopes can be stuffed with almost any cheesy filling.

15

Makes 6-8

PANCAKE CRITTERS

You'll Need

1½ C. all-purpose flour
3 T. sugar
1 T. baking powder
¼ tsp. salt
2 eggs
1 C. buttermilk
¼ C. milk
½ tsp. vanilla

3 T. butter, melted
Critter details *(blueberries, strawberries, grapes, chocolate chips, mini marshmallows and M&Ms, almonds, crisp bacon strips, etc.)*
Ready-to-use frosting, optional
Maple syrup
Squeeze bottle, optional

1 In one bowl, whisk together flour, sugar, baking powder, and salt; set aside. In another bowl, whisk the eggs until foamy, then whisk in the buttermilk, milk, and vanilla.

2 Add melted butter to the milk mixture and stir well. Pour it into the set-aside flour mixture and stir everything together to make a thick batter *(it may still be lumpy)*. Pour some batter into a squeeze bottle, if using, or get out a ladle or dry measuring cup with a handle.

3 Preheat a large nonstick griddle or skillet over medium heat. Squeeze or scoop batter onto the griddle, making big and little circles and other shapes. Cook until bottoms are golden brown. Flip carefully and cook another minute.

4 Cut some circles in half or quarters to make ears, noses, or feet. Layer the pancake pieces on a plate and fasten together with a dab of frosting. Add whatever details you like. Drizzle with syrup and eat 'em up!

Spoon frosting into a plastic baggie and cut off one corner. Squeeze frosting out of the bag to glue your pancake pieces together.

ZUCCHINI TORPEDO BOATS

You'll Need

- 4 medium zucchini
- ½ lb. ground turkey
- 1 tsp. salt
- ½ tsp. each garlic powder, ground cumin, chili powder, and paprika
- ¼ tsp. ground oregano
- 1 C. prepared rice*
- ½ C. chickpeas *(garbanzo beans)*, drained & rinsed
- ½ C. shredded Colby-Jack cheese, plus more for topping
- ½ C. salsa
- Melon baller *(recommended)*
- Mini bell peppers, cheese slices, pretzel sticks, and/or cream cheese
- Long toothpicks, optional

Makes 8

1 Trim off the ends of zucchini. Slice in half lengthwise **(adult's job)** and use a melon baller or spoon to scoop out the seeds to create ½"-thick shells *(your boats)*. Microwave the shells on high 4 to 5 minutes, just to soften. Let cool enough to touch.

2 In a skillet over medium heat, brown the turkey until cooked and crumbly; stir in all the seasonings, then let the mixture cool slightly. Meanwhile, preheat your oven's broiler.

3 In a big bowl, stir together the rice, chickpeas, ½ C. cheese, salsa, and turkey mixture. Spoon filling into each boat and sprinkle with more cheese. Set on a broiler pan and broil 4" from heat about 6 minutes, until lightly browned.

4 To make flags, halve bell peppers and poke with a long toothpick, or attach triangles of cheese to pretzel sticks with a bit of cream cheese. Raise a flag in each boat!

> ** For fast magic use 1 (4.4 oz.) tub ready-to-serve microwavable brown rice from an 8.8 oz. package.*

SERVINGS VARY

FREEZER FACES

Large oranges
Chocolate ice cream or lime sherbet
Mike and Ike candies
Grapefruit knife *(recommended)*

1 Cut off the top of one orange for each face you want to make. With a grapefruit knife or paring knife and spoon, hollow out the pulp to leave a thick orange shell **(adult's job)**.

2 Draw a jack-o-lantern or monster face on one side of each orange shell with a marker. Using a sharp knife, carefully cut out the pieces as drawn **(adult's job)**. Cut one or more small holes in the removed top.

3 Pack scoops of ice cream or sherbet into the shells and set the tops back on. Insert candies into the hole(s) for the pumpkin stem or monster hair and horns. Eat right away or freeze at least 3 hours.

That orange pulp you removed? Eat it up now or add it to a fruit salad.

STRAWBERRY ROLL-UPS

Preheat your oven to its lowest temperature *(140° to 170°*)*. Line a large rimmed baking sheet with a silicone baking mat *(or use high-quality plastic wrap, but no parchment paper, foil, or waxed paper)*. In a food processor, puree 3 C. sliced fresh strawberries with 2 T. sugar and 1 tsp. lemon juice until very smooth **(adult's job)**. Spread on the silicone mat into a rectangle about ⅛" thick *(avoid edges and don't spread too thin)*. Place pan in oven to bake 6 to 8 hours* or until center is dry to the touch and no longer tacky. Remove from oven and peel slightly warm strawberry leather off the silicone. With a pizza cutter or kitchen shears, cut into squares or long strips while warm; roll promptly in waxed or parchment paper. Reheat as needed for easy rolling. Store in an airtight container.

* *If baking at 170°, turn the oven off and on every 30 minutes for best results.*

Makes 10

CHICKEN LOGS

MAKES 16

You'll Need

1 (17.3 oz.) pkg. frozen puff pastry sheets *(2 ct.)*

Day-old bread or buns

1 medium carrot, peeled

1 medium zucchini

¾ C. finely chopped onion

1 tsp. minced garlic

1 lb. ground chicken

1 tsp. garlic salt

½ tsp. black pepper

2 eggs, divided

3 T. milk, divided

Sesame seed

> When this pastry bakes, it magically puffs up and separates into tons of flaky layers. How many can you see?

1. Thaw the pastry sheets following package directions *(about 40 minutes)*. Meanwhile, tear the bread into little pieces to measure 1½ C. Finely grate the carrot into a big bowl. Grate the zucchini and drain on paper towels. Line baking sheets with parchment paper and preheat your oven to 375°.

> Always wash hands well before handling food. Then rip up that bread!

2. Add the torn bread, zucchini, onion, garlic, chicken, garlic salt, and pepper to the bowl with the carrot and mix well – really dig in there with your hands! Add 1 egg and 1 T. milk and mix some more.

3. Cut the pastry sheets into four even pieces. Spread some of the chicken mixture *(about ½ C.)* down the center of each pastry piece. Wrap the pastry around the filling, pinching edges together to seal. Cut the logs in half and set on the prepped pans, seam side down.

4. In a small bowl, mix the remaining egg and 2 T. milk. Brush the egg wash over the rolls and sprinkle with sesame seed. Bake 35 minutes or until golden brown. Serve warm with sweet and sour sauce or barbecue sauce.

SPAGHETTI & CANNONBALLS

SERVES 6-8

You'll Need

1 C. dry bread crumbs

½ C. grated Parmesan cheese

1 T. dried parsley

1 tsp. salt

½ tsp. black pepper

½ tsp. dried thyme

¼ tsp. garlic powder

¼ tsp. ground oregano

2 eggs

1 lb. ground beef

½ lb. ground sausage

1 lb. uncooked spaghetti noodles

1 (24 oz.) jar spaghetti sauce

Shredded Parmesan cheese

*Make a **Funny Face Salad** with a wedge of lettuce, tomato slice, 2 celery slices with blueberry eyeballs, a summer squash nose, and an orange bell pepper mouth. Serve with ranch dressing.*

24

1 Preheat your oven to 375° and lightly grease a broiler pan. In a big bowl, mix the bread crumbs, ½ C. cheese, parsley, salt, pepper, thyme, garlic powder, and oregano.

Use big bowls instead of small ones so kids can mix ingredients without spilling everything over the sides.

2 Add the eggs, beef, and sausage. Then get in there with your hands and smoosh it all together.

3 Roll the mixture into 1½" balls. Set them on the prepped pan and bake 20 to 25 minutes or until cooked through.

4 Meanwhile, break the noodles in half and cook them in a pot of boiling water as directed on the package; drain **(adult's job)**. Heat the sauce in a saucepan.

5 Pile some spaghetti, a few cannonballs, and some sauce on each plate and sprinkle with shredded Parmesan. Serve with your salad masterpiece!

STRAWBERRY CLOUD PARFAITS

Soften 4 oz. cream cheese and beat on medium speed until smooth. Beat in 1 (8 oz.) tub of whipped topping *(thawed)* until well mixed; stir in 1½ tsp. clear vanilla and set aside. Unmold 4 snack cups of strawberry gelatin *(we used a 13 oz. package)* and cut into ½" cubes with a table knife – the cubes don't have to be perfect. Spoon or pipe a layer of the cream cheese mixture into 4 (7 to 8 oz.) parfait glasses or dessert dishes. Add a layer of gelatin cubes and sliced fresh strawberries, then repeat the layers. Top with leftover cream cheese mixture or whipped cream and more berries. Parfait perfection! *(Try other delicious combos, like berry blue or lemon gelatin with blueberries, raspberry gelatin with raspberries, or peach gelatin with diced peaches.)*

CARAMEL CRUNCH BARS

MAKES 12

Butter

4 to 5 whole graham crackers

1 (11 oz.) pkg. caramel bits

2 T. heavy cream

½ C. salted dry roasted peanuts

½ C. mini marshmallows

½ C. broken pretzels

½ C. Snickers Bites or mini M&Ms

¼ C. semi-sweet chocolate chips

1 to 2 tsp. shortening

1 Line an 8 x 8" pan with foil, letting foil extend over two sides. Coat foil with butter. Cover bottom of pan with crackers, cutting as needed to fit.

2 Microwave the caramel bits with cream for 2 minutes until melted and smooth, stirring every 30 seconds **(adult's job)**. Pour over crackers in pan.

3 Sprinkle with peanuts, marshmallows, pretzels, and Snickers Bites, pressing gently.

4 Melt the chocolate chips and shortening in the microwave, stirring until smooth **(adult's job)**. Drizzle over the panful of goodness and then chill at least 1 hour. Remove from pan by lifting the foil. Cut into bars.

FIESTA LETTUCE WRAPS

MAKES 12

You'll Need

- 1 lb. ground beef
- 3 T. taco seasoning
- ¼ C. water
- 1 C. frozen corn, thawed
- 1 (15 oz.) can black beans, drained & rinsed
- ½ C. ranch dressing
- 1 tsp. ground cumin
- 1 tsp. garlic powder
- ½ tsp. salt
- 12 large leaf, butterhead, or Romaine lettuce leaves, rinsed & drained *(or use warm flour tortillas instead)*
- 1 medium tomato, diced
- 1 avocado, peeled & diced
- ½ C. diced green bell pepper

1. In a big skillet over medium heat, brown the ground beef until cooked and crumbly; drain **(adult's job)**. Stir in taco seasoning and water. Add the corn and beans and simmer over low heat.

2. Meanwhile, in a spouted measuring cup, whisk together the dressing, cumin, garlic powder, and salt.

3. Scoop about ⅓ C. of the meat mixture onto each lettuce leaf. Dress it up with tomato, avocado, bell pepper, and/or ranch mixture, any way you like it.

4. Fold the leafy end of the lettuce up and over the filling and then fold in both sides to make a taco-filled pocket; fasten with a pick as needed. Pick it up and gobble down!

Want lettuce boats instead? Skip the wrapping and just scoop everything onto big lettuce leaves. You'll want to use a fork to eat it!

Makes 12

ICE CREAM SANDWICHES

You'll Need

- ¼ C. shortening
- ¼ C. butter, softened
- ½ C. creamy peanut butter
- ½ C. brown sugar
- ½ C. sugar, plus more for rolling
- 1 egg
- 1 C. all-purpose flour
- ¼ C. whole wheat flour
- ¾ tsp. baking soda
- ½ tsp. baking powder
- ¼ tsp. salt
- 1 qt. vanilla or chocolate ice cream
- Candy sprinkles and/or mini chocolate chips, optional

1 Preheat your oven to 375° and line cookie sheets with parchment paper. In a big bowl, beat shortening and butter on medium speed until creamy. Beat in peanut butter, brown sugar, ½ C. sugar, and egg.

2 Add both flours, baking soda, baking powder, and salt to bowl and beat until dough forms. Shape the dough into 1¼" balls and roll them in sugar.

3 Set balls 3" apart on the prepped pans. Flatten with a fork in a crisscross pattern. Bake 9 to 11 minutes, until lightly browned. Cool completely.

4 Press a scoop of ice cream between two cookies. Roll the edges in sprinkles or chips if you'd like. Set on a rimmed pan and freeze until firm. Wrap in plastic wrap to store.

Serves 4-6

STUFFED CRUST PIZZA

You'll Need

- 3 C. biscuit baking mix
- ⅔ C. hot water
- 2 T. olive oil
- ¾ C. diced pepperoni, divided
- 4 sticks mozzarella string cheese
- ¾ to 1 C. pizza sauce
- 2 C. shredded Italian cheese blend, divided
- Your favorite pizza toppings

1. Preheat your oven to 450° and grease a 12" pizza pan. In a big bowl, stir together the baking mix, water, and oil until a soft dough forms. Then beat vigorously 20 times. Cover and let stand 8 minutes.

2. Press dough into the prepped pan, making edge extend 1" over the side of pan. Scatter ¼ C. pepperoni around edge of dough. Tear cheese sticks in half lengthwise to get eight pieces and set them on the pepperoni.

3. Fold the extended edge of dough toward the center to wrap the cheese and pepperoni inside the crust; press well to seal. Bake the crust for 7 minutes.

Look for the magic. After baking, those cheese sticks will melt into ooey-gooey goodness!

4. Spread sauce over partially baked crust and sprinkle with half the shredded cheese, remaining pepperoni, and other toppings; sprinkle with remaining shredded cheese. Bake 9 to 12 minutes longer or until crust is golden brown.

Makes 24

CORN DOG BITES

You'll Need

- 4 to 5 hot dogs
- ¼ C. butter, melted
- ¼ C. sugar
- 1 egg
- ½ C. buttermilk
- ½ C. all-purpose flour
- ½ C. cornmeal
- ¼ tsp. baking soda
- ¼ tsp. salt

Use a cutting board to protect your countertop when cutting.

1. Preheat your oven to 375° and coat 24 mini muffin cups with cooking spray. Cut the hot dogs into 1" pieces and set aside.

2. Pour the butter and sugar into a medium bowl and whisk together. Whisk in the egg. Add the buttermilk and stir well.

3. In another bowl, whisk together the flour, cornmeal, baking soda, and salt. Add the buttermilk mixture and stir until blended.

4. Spoon 1 T. batter into each prepped muffin cup. Press one hot dog piece into the middle of each cup. Bake 9 to 13 minutes or until light golden brown. Cool 5 minutes before removing from pan. Serve with ketchup and mustard for dipping.

MAKES 14-16

S'MORES KRISPIE ROLLS

¼ C. butter

1 (10 oz.) pkg. mini marshmallows

5 C. crisp rice cereal

1 (7 oz.) container marshmallow crème

¾ to 1 C. graham cracker crumbs

1 C. semi-sweet chocolate chips

2 tsp. coconut oil

1 Line a 10 x 15" rimmed baking sheet with waxed paper and spritz with cooking spray.

2 Put butter and marshmallows in a big microwaveable bowl and microwave on high for 2 minutes, stirring every minute until smooth **(adult's job)**. Stir in the cereal until well coated.

3 With buttered hands, press mixture into the prepped pan, making a thin even layer. Spread with marshmallow crème and sprinkle with cracker crumbs; press lightly to hold.

4 Melt chocolate chips and oil in the microwave, stirring until smooth. Spread chocolate over the layers in pan. Slice in half lengthwise. Starting from a long side, roll each half into a log; chill 1 hour. Slice into 1" rounds to serve.

 Watch those marshmallows puff up in the microwave. It's almost like they're alive!

Serves 2-4

WAFFLED SWEET POTATOES

Preheat your waffle iron on high, then coat with cooking spray (adult's job). Spread 2 to 2½ C. frozen *(thawed)* sweet potato fries on a big piece of waxed paper. In a small bowl, mix ⅛ tsp. cinnamon, ¼ tsp. black pepper, and ¼ to ½ tsp. each salt, garlic powder, smoked paprika, and dried oregano. Sprinkle the mixture over the fries and toss gently with your hands to coat. Pile the fries on the iron, making a thick, even layer (adult's job) and close the lid firmly. Cook until golden brown and crisp, 2 to 3 minutes, pressing down on the handle with a hot pad so all the fries are cooked. Remove from iron and serve plain or with butter and syrup.

BAKED VEGGIE BITES

SERVES 4

You'll Need

⅓ C. butter, melted, divided

1 egg

2 tsp. water

½ C. all-purpose flour

½ tsp. salt

Black pepper to taste

¼ tsp. paprika

2 to 3 C. fresh vegetable pieces *(try broccoli or cauliflower florets, baby carrots, halved mini bell peppers, and ½" zucchini slices)*

Grated Parmesan cheese, optional

Go ahead and dip these little gems into ranch dressing – they're delicious!

1. Preheat the oven to 450°. Brush the bottom of a 9 x 13" pan with about 1 T. of the melted butter.

2. In a shallow dish, whisk together the egg and water. Mix the flour, salt, pepper, and paprika in another shallow dish.

> Place your hands over theirs to guide kids through trickier tasks.

3. One piece at a time, dip vegetables into the egg mixture, then roll in the flour mixture to coat. Set in a single layer in the prepped pan. Pour the remaining butter over vegetable pieces.

4. Bake uncovered for 10 minutes, then flip the pieces over **(adult's job)**. Bake 6 to 9 minutes more or until tender and lightly browned. Sprinkle lightly with Parmesan cheese if you'd like.

Makes 1½ cups

MR. GREEN DIP

Thaw and shell 1 (10 oz.) bag frozen edamame; discard shells and dump the beans into a food processor container. Add ¾ C. frozen *(thawed)* sweet green peas, 2 tsp. minced garlic, ¼ C. sliced green onion, 2½ T. chopped flat-leaf parsley, 1 T. chopped fresh mint, and 3 T. creamy Italian dressing. Puree until well blended **(adult's job)**. Add 3 T. lemon juice, 1½ T. each honey and olive oil, and ¼ tsp. each salt and black pepper. Process until nearly smooth. Transfer to a serving bowl and create Mr. Green's face on top using sliced olives, mini bell peppers, and chopped parsley. Is your fella silly or scary? Dip in with pita chips, whole grain crackers, or fresh vegetables like carrots and celery.

Makes 1⅓ cups

NUTTY CHOCOLATE FONDUE

In the top of a double boiler or a saucepan set over a pan of simmering water, heat 1 C. heavy cream until it simmers **(adult's job)**. Add 1 C. milk chocolate chips and let stand until softened, about 1 minute; whisk until melted and smooth. Gradually whisk in ½ C. crunchy peanut butter until blended. Transfer to a heat-proof bowl and serve with dippers such as pretzels, mini donuts, small brownies, sliced bananas, angel food cake chunks, and/or cookie halves *(the peanut butter cookies from page 30 are delish)*.

Serves 4

LIL' SMOKY CALZONE

Preheat your oven to 425°. Cook 5 bacon strips in the microwave until crisp, 4 to 5 minutes **(adult's job)**; drain on paper towels and crumble. Unroll 1 *(10 to 13.8 oz.)* tube refrigerated pizza crust on an ungreased baking sheet and press it into a 12" circle. On half of the dough circle, sprinkle ¾ C. shredded mozzarella cheese and 8 sliced little smoky sausages to within ½" of the outer edge; top with ¾ C. shredded cheddar cheese and the crumbled bacon. Fold the plain side of dough over the filling and pinch the edges together to seal well. Brush lightly with a beaten egg and sprinkle with sea salt if you'd like. Bake 11 to 15 minutes or until golden brown. Cut into wedges to serve.

PB ROLO BALLS

MAKES 12-15

- 2 C. corn flakes cereal
- 2 T. sugar
- ¾ C. creamy peanut butter
- ⅓ C. light corn syrup
- 12-15 Rolo candies
- Powdered sugar, optional
- 1¼ C. milk chocolate chips, optional
- 1½ T. shortening, optional

1 Pour corn flakes into a large zippered plastic bag and crush with a rolling pin; dump the crumbs into a big bowl. Add the sugar, peanut butter, and corn syrup; mix well.

2 Roll the mixture into 1½" balls, then tuck a Rolo candy inside each ball. Be sure it's covered well. Chill 30 minutes.

3 For white balls, roll them in powdered sugar and let set a few minutes before rolling again.

4 For chocolate-covered balls, microwave the chocolate chips and shortening, stirring until melted and smooth. Coat the chilled balls in chocolate, letting the excess drip off. Let dry on waxed paper.

It's smart to wear an apron when tasks are messy.

43

Makes 12

BANANA CRUNCH MUFFINS

You'll Need

- 3 very ripe medium bananas
- ⅓ C. brown sugar
- ½ tsp. cinnamon
- 2 T. plus 1½ C. all-purpose flour, divided
- 1 T. cold butter
- 1 tsp. baking soda
- 1 tsp. baking powder
- ½ tsp. salt
- ¾ C. sugar
- ⅓ C. butter, melted
- 1 egg
- ½ C. chopped fresh strawberries, optional
- Ice cream scoop *(recommended)*

44

1. Preheat your oven to 375°. Line 12 muffin cups with cupcake liners. Use a fork to mash the bananas in a shallow bowl until really smooshed up; set aside.

2. To make the topping, stir together the brown sugar, cinnamon, and 2 T. flour in a small bowl; cut in the cold butter until crumbly. Set topping aside.

See how the packed brown sugar holds the shape of the measuring cup? Perfectly done.

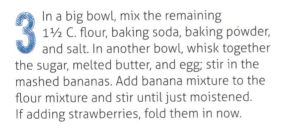

3. In a big bowl, mix the remaining 1½ C. flour, baking soda, baking powder, and salt. In another bowl, whisk together the sugar, melted butter, and egg; stir in the mashed bananas. Add banana mixture to the flour mixture and stir until just moistened. If adding strawberries, fold them in now.

4. Use an ice cream scoop or large spoon to spoon batter into the liners, filling each about ¾ full. Sprinkle the set-aside topping over muffins and bake 18 to 20 minutes or until they test done with a toothpick.

ELEPHANT EARS

MAKES 4

You'll Need

1 C. all-purpose flour
Sugar
½ tsp. baking powder
½ tsp. salt
⅓ C. milk
¼ C. butter, melted, divided
1 tsp. cinnamon

Want shiny glazed ears? Microwave 1 T. water and 3 T. sugar until dissolved; cool slightly, then brush over the warm pastries. Ele-phantastic!

1 Preheat your oven to 425° and line a big cookie sheet with parchment paper.

2 In a medium bowl, mix the flour, 2 T. sugar, baking powder, and salt with a big spoon. Stir in the milk and 3 T. melted butter until dough forms. Place the dough on a floured surface and knead 10 times *(count 'em!)*. With a rolling pin, flatten the dough into a 5 x 9" rectangle. Brush with the remaining 1 T. melted butter.

3 In a small bowl, mix the cinnamon with 3 T. sugar; sprinkle over the buttered dough. Beginning at one short side, roll the dough into a log and pinch the edge to seal well. Cut the log into four equal slices with unflavored dental floss or a sharp knife.

4 Set slices on the prepped cookie sheet and press flat to make 5" to 6" circles. Sprinkle with more sugar and bake 10 to 15 minutes, until lightly browned. Cool slightly before devouring.

Go ahead – use both hands to squash these dough circles flat!

FRUIT SALSA WITH CINNAMON CRISPS

You'll Need

6 to 7 large flour tortillas
Cooking spray
½ C. plus 1 tsp. sugar, divided
1 T. cinnamon
1 lb. fresh strawberries

2 fresh mangoes or peaches
3 kiwifruit
¾ C. fresh blueberries
2 tsp. lime juice
1 tsp. lime zest

1 Preheat your oven to 375° and line baking sheets with foil. One at a time, spray the tortillas with cooking spray.

2 In a bowl, whisk together ½ C. sugar and the cinnamon. Sprinkle the cinnamon-sugar mixture evenly over the tortillas.

A table knife works great to cut most soft fruits.

3 With a pizza cutter, slice the tortillas into wedges and set them on the prepped baking sheets. Bake 6 to 8 minutes, until lightly browned and crispy. Let cool.

4 Meanwhile, hull the strawberries and peel the mangoes and kiwis. Cut out the mango pits **(adult's job)**. Chop the fruit and put it in a big bowl. Add blueberries, lime juice, zest, and remaining 1 tsp. sugar; stir and let rest a few minutes. Dip into that salsa with your yummy chips!

MAKES 30

STUFFED CHIPPERS

½ C. butter, softened
½ C. sugar
¼ C. plus 2 T. brown sugar
1 egg
1½ tsp. vanilla
1¾ C. all-purpose flour
½ tsp. salt
½ tsp. baking soda
1 C. mini chocolate chips
30 mini Oreo cookies

1. Preheat your oven to 350° and line cookie sheets with parchment paper.

2. In a big mixing bowl, beat together the butter, sugar, and brown sugar on medium speed until creamy. Beat in the egg and vanilla.

3. In a small bowl, combine the flour, salt, and baking soda. Add to the butter mixture and beat well. Stir in the chocolate chips with a spoon.

4. Make 30 mounds of dough on the prepped cookie sheets, using 1 level tablespoon for each; set aside remainder. Press an Oreo into each mound and top with a teaspoonful of remaining dough. Pinch edges together to seal the Oreo inside.

5. Bake 11 to 14 minutes, until lightly browned. Cool slightly, then transfer to a cooling rack.

SHAKE IT UP RANCH SNACK

In a big paper grocery sack, combine 1 (7 oz.) box Cheez-It or Goldfish Crackers, 1 (8 to 9 oz.) pkg. oyster crackers, 1 (9 oz.) can cashews, 1 (7.5 oz.) bag Bugles snacks, and 1 (16 oz.) bag small pretzels. In a spouted bowl, whisk together ¾ to 1 C. canola oil, 2 (1 oz.) pkgs. dry ranch dressing mix, and optional 2 T. dill weed. Drizzle over the cracker combo and roll the sack closed; shake it, shake it, shake it to coat everything. Spread on paper towels to dry at room temperature, or divide among two parchment paper-lined baking sheets and bake at 325° for 10 to 15 minutes, then spread on paper towels to cool. Store in airtight containers or divide among individual bags for party favors.

RISE & SHINE BURRITOS

You'll Need

4 frozen hash brown patties
Salt and black pepper to taste
6 eggs
1 T. water
2 tsp. butter

4 (8") flour tortillas
1 C. shredded cheddar cheese
½ green bell pepper, diced
½ C. bacon bits or crumbled cooked bacon

1. Preheat your oven to 350°. Follow package directions to microwave or pan fry the hash brown patties **(adult's job)**. Season with salt and pepper.

2. Whisk the eggs with water until light. Melt the butter in a big skillet over medium-low heat and add the eggs. Cook until set but still shiny, stirring often.

3. Set each tortilla on a 12" square of foil. Crumble a cooked hash brown patty in the center of each tortilla. Divide the cooked eggs, cheese, bell pepper, and bacon evenly over the hash browns.

4. Fold two opposite sides of the tortilla over the filling, then roll up burrito-style; wrap the foil snugly around each one. Bake 20 to 25 minutes or until hot and melty.

Use oven mitts or hot pads to handle hot things.

53

Makes 2

DOUBLE DECKER DUDES

You'll Need

3 slices whole grain bread, divided

Soft butter

2 slices white cheese, divided *(we used provolone)*

1 small cucumber

2 slices black forest ham

2 stuffed green olives, one end trimmed

2 black olives, closed end trimmed

1 slice salami

3" cookie cutters

1. FROG: Cut two 3" rounds of bread with a cookie cutter. Spread one side with butter. Cut a 3" sunshine shape from a slice of cheese. Cut 3" off the end of cucumber and slice lengthwise into a thin tongue shape **(adult's job)**.

2. To assemble, layer ham and cheese shape on one bread round with cuke tongue in the middle, rounded end sticking out. Top with remaining bread round. Fasten green olive eyes on top with butter.

3. MONSTER: Cut four ½" strips from remaining cheese slice. Cut two thin cucumber rounds. Fill black olive holes with a bit of cheese. Toast remaining slice of bread and spread with butter; cut diagonally into two triangles.

4. To assemble, set salami on one buttered side of toast, sticking out beyond cut edge like a tongue. Line up cheese strips on tongue like teeth and top with the other toast triangle. Set cucumber rounds on top with olives in the middle to look like eyes.

TOTS GRILLED CHEESE

Serves 1

Defrost 18 frozen tater tots. In a big nonstick skillet or griddle *(not on the heat yet)*, arrange nine tots side by side in three rows to make a rectangle. Make a second rectangle with the other nine tots in the remaining skillet space. With a spatula or your hands, press down on the rectangles to make two flat patties. Set the skillet over medium heat **(adult's job)** and cook until bottoms begin to crisp, 3 to 5 minutes. Set a thin slice of cheese on each rectangle and sprinkle with ¼ C. of your favorite shredded cheese(s) *(we used white cheddar slices with shredded longhorn and mozzarella)*. Cover the pan and cook until cheese melts. Carefully flip one cheesy rectangle onto the other to form a sandwich, cheese sides together. Press lightly and cook just until crisp on both sides.

SERVES 8

COTTON CANDY ICE CREAM

- 3 C. heavy cream
- 1 (11 oz.) can sweetened condensed milk
- 1 tsp. vanilla *(or other favorite flavoring)*
- Food coloring
- Candy sprinkles, optional

1 In a big chilled mixing bowl with chilled beaters, beat the cream on high speed until almost stiff peaks form. Fold in the sweetened condensed milk and vanilla until well blended.

2 Divide the mixture among five bowls. Stir a different food coloring into four bowls and leave one white.

3 Layer dollops of alternating colors in a 5 x 9" loaf pan. Tap the pan lightly on the counter to remove air bubbles *(don't stir)*. Top with sprinkles if you'd like; cover and freeze at least 5 hours.

4 Let soften slightly before scooping into cones or bowls.

Use plenty of food coloring if you like bright colors. Mix your own fun tints, too!

Serves 1

HOME FOR LUNCH

You'll Need

Peanut butter

1 slice whole wheat bread

1 slice American cheese

Chex cereal squares

Mini chocolate chips

3 celery sticks, divided

½ stick mozzarella string cheese

2 slices summer squash or zucchini

2 fresh sugar snap peas

2 grape tomatoes

Thin wooden skewers and toothpicks

1 **House:** Spread peanut butter on bread and set on a large plate; remove crusts. Slice the cheese in half diagonally and set one triangle above the bread for a roof. Cut a door shape from remaining cheese and set in place.

2 Attach cereal squares as windows. Add a chocolate chip doorknob and a short celery stick chimney.

3 **Person:** Peel apart one end of the cheese stick to look like a head with hair. Thread squash slices on a wooden skewer *(body)*. Thread the head end of cheese onto the skewer above the body.

4 Attach snap pea arms and celery stick legs to the body with toothpicks. Use half-toothpicks to fasten tomato feet to the legs. Press chocolate chip eyes into the cheese face. Take your new friend home for lunch!

MAKES 24

LITTLE DIPPERS

¼ C. grated Parmesan cheese

½ tsp. Italian seasoning

1 (11 oz.) tube refrigerated breadsticks

1 C. pizza sauce

¼ C. shredded mozzarella cheese

1. Preheat your oven to 375°. Dump the Parmesan cheese and Italian seasoning into a big zippered plastic bag; seal and shake until mixed.

2. Unroll and separate the breadsticks. Cut each one in half crosswise with a table knife. Add the dough pieces to the bag, a few at a time, seal bag, and shake gently to coat.

3. Arrange the pieces on an ungreased cookie sheet and bake 10 to 13 minutes or until golden brown.

4. Heat the pizza sauce in the microwave for 1 to 2 minutes or until bubbly. Sprinkle with mozzarella and microwave 1 minute more to melt the cheese. Serve with the breadsticks.

Divide the sauce among small cups so everyone gets their own. Then you can double dip!